STUDEBAKER
Less Than They Promised

STUDEBAKER
Less Than They Promised

MICHAEL BEATTY
PATRICK FURLONG
LOREN PENNINGTON

and books

SOUTH BEND, INDIANA

and books
702 South Michigan, South Bend, Indiana 46618

Library of Congress Catalog Number: 84-081548

International Standard Book Number: 0-89708-129-3

1 2 3 4 5 6 7 8 9

Printed in the United States of America

Additional copies available:
     the distributors
     702 South Michigan
     South Bend, Indiana 46618

Designer: Catherine Dinsmore

Acknowledgments

I would like to express my gratitude and appreciation to the following:

Kathy Giangreco, Robert Schneiger, Greg Sinn, Robin Rutledge, Steve Cardwell, Rick Coken, Steve Robbins, Dave Moyer, Charles Lawson, Mike Moyer, Dunlap Sims and Howard Smogor.

Researchers Julie Bennett, Geoffrey Huys, Marsha Mullin, Carl Tuveson, Bob Harrison, Jim Kelly, and Chris Buchman. Also Ruth Ross, Patti Foos, Betty Stepniewski, Caryll Vicsik and all the community members who gave of their time and materials.

The following organizations and their staffs: Discovery Hall Museum and The Studebaker Muse-um, WNIT-TV, Indiana University at South Bend, WBBM-TV, The Studebaker Driver's Club, WNDU-TV, The University of Notre Dame, and the South Bend Tribune.

I would also like to thank the people of *and books*, Catherine Dinsmore, and, for their outstanding contribution throughout the project, I would like to thank Dr. Patrick Furlong, and Dr. Loren Pennington.

Finally, I would like to thank Scott Craig for his direction, professionalism and receptivity; and the Indiana Committee for the Humanities for their support of the project.

Michael Beatty
Editor
July, 1984

INTRODUCTION

A one hundred eleven year relationship, one comparable to marriage in many respects, existed between the Studebaker Corporation and the community of South Bend, Indiana. Although not the only employer in town—by 1963 when it closed automotive operations, it wasn't even the primary one—the community always associated itself with the company. Through its wagons—by the turn of the century the company was reputed to be the world's largest manufacturer—and later through its cars, Studebaker gave the city a world reputation. However, not all that renown was positive. Some say prospective employers stayed away because of wage and labor problems that arose from Studebaker's relationship with its workers. But an article in **Life Magazine** praised the quality of that relationship; and the United Auto Workers organized and worked peacefully with management for thirty years before 'outsiders' in the form of Packard management forced strikes in the 1950s. There were lean years, even a receivership for the company in 1933, but the city and company continued to grow and depend on each other through good and bad turns, until December 9, 1963 when Studebaker closed its automotive plant in South Bend.

The initial reaction was one of shock. But the automotive company had been ailing for years, and the shock was similar to that felt when a family member finally succumbs after a lingering illness. Times were good and the city recovered, and recovered quickly. Though scarred, two years after the shut down South Bend's unemployment was down to 2.5% and, according to national publications of that time, the city was in excellent economic health with a labor shortage as its major problem. Twenty years after the automotive line stopped workers still remember the company with fondness: "We were always proud to work for Studebaker."

In some ways Studebaker, South Bend, and the people can be considered a case study, an example, a microcosm for events that happened and are happening to other companies, other communities, and other workers. Many questions about the company are still unanswered. Could the automotive division of Studebaker have continued? Who was responsible for its demise? What was the responsibility to the community in which Studebaker existed? What lessons can this shutdown teach other communities? How were the company and community influenced by events outside of their control, events such as national and international politics, war and peace, social welfare and changing work ethics, immigration, changing tastes, and changing incomes?

There are no simple answers to these questions, and we don't attempt that here. Our hope is to offer a springboard for thought, discussion and further investigation. We would be happy to hear from you with your thoughts and ideas on these topics and can be reached through the publisher.

THE STUDEBAKER BROTHERS.

CLEM STUDEBAKER   HENRY STUDEBAKER   J. M. STUDEBAKER
PETER E. STUDEBAKER   J. F. STUDEBAKER

I.
Beginnings
through World War 2

PATRICK FURLONG, PhD

The Beginnings

The Studebaker family's westward journey is a familiar story of the American frontier. Raised in the German Dunkard tradition in Gettysburg, Pennsylvania, they moved west to Ashland, Ohio, in a Conestoga wagon they built for themselves, seeking greater opportunity and a more prosperous way of life. They were good, hard-working, religious people, and for generations the men of the family had worked as blacksmiths and wagon builders, with some farming on the side. In 1849 John Studebaker traveled over much of Ohio and Indiana, seeking a growing town where he could settle with his wife Rebecca and their family of five sons and five daughters. He chose South Bend as a likely place with good prospects for the future. The second son, 19 year old Clement, moved first to prepare the way for the rest of the family. Clem saw ample supplies of oak and hickory as he traveled through northern Indiana, and the iron fittings for a wagon he knew his family could shape in the blacksmith shop, but, like so many pioneers, the Studebaker family lacked the cash to establish themselves in business.

Clem Studebaker taught school for a year, worked in a blacksmith shop, and saved his wages. He was soon joined by his older brother Henry and by February of 1852 they had enough money to open their own blacksmith shop. John and Rebecca Studebaker and their eight remaining children came to South Bend in the family's Pennsylvania-built Conestoga wagon, but John was not well enough to swing hammer against anvil any longer.

The sons loyally supported their parents in increasing comfort for more than a quarter of a century.

The two Studebaker brothers operated a general blacksmithing business. They made and fitted horseshoes, repaired broken farm and household utensils, produced a variety of small iron products, and they also built wagons on demand. Their entire starting capital was $68, and during their first year in business they manufactured only two wagons. There was an ample supply of the necessary hardwood in the South Bend area, and the iron fittings for a wagon were well within the capability of any good blacksmith. According to family tradition the Studebaker motto was "Always Give the Customer More Than You Promised," a slogan which their successors would advertise proudly for more than a century. Some persons have said the motto really was "Always Give the Customer a Little More Than You Promised," because giving too much would eliminate the profit and soon bankrupt the business.

Like most small businessmen, the Studebaker brothers were limited by their lack of capital. They did receive a lucky contract in 1857 for 100 army wagons from George Milburn's wagon factory in Mishawaka, which could not deliver the large order he had promised the government. Henry and Clem Studebaker hired extra workmen and built a drying kiln to season the needed timber quickly, and delivered the wagons in ninety days of hectic effort. This showed the possibilities of large scale production, but the Studebakers still did not have enough money to expand as they wished.

Artist rendering of the Studebaker Brothers' father, John Studebaker, and his blacksmith shop in Pennsylvania.

First Studebaker office and carriage works in South Bend. The shop was opened on February 16, 1852.

In 1858 help came just at the right moment when their younger brother John Mohler Studebaker returned from his adventures in the California gold fields. He had not found any gold, but he had prospered by making wheelbarrows for the miners and he arrived in South Bend with eight thousand dollars in cash. Henry decided that he preferred to be a full-time farmer and so sold his interest in the firm to John M. and retired from the business.

From the Civil War To the Largest Wagon Maker In the World

The Civil War brought an abundance of army orders for wagons, artillery caissons, and other vehicles. Studebaker wagons held up well under the difficulties of army service, and many soldiers were eager to buy a quality Studebaker farm wagon when they returned to civilian life. Peter Studebaker joined his brothers in 1863 and became the firm's chief salesman, travelling the country to build up a network of dealers, something no other wagon manufacturer had ever attempted. Peter had opened the first Studebaker 'dealership' himself three years earlier next to his general store in Goshen, Indiana, about 20 miles from South Bend. Clem was the general manager, John M. was in charge of production, and Peter signed a simple contract to describe his duties: "I, Peter Studebaker, agree to sell all the wagons my brother Clem can make." Clem added simply, "I agree to make all he can sell." Peter traveled throughout the United States, but particularly in the growing West where wagons were most in demand. The first 'wagon repository' of branch sales office and warehouse was located in St. Joseph, Missouri, the starting place for many wagon trains across the Plains to California and Oregon. When the railroad was completed to California in 1869 the Studebakers began to ship their wagons west by rail, often in carload lots. Peter visited San Francisco in 1870 and set up a dealership there to deal exclusively in Studebaker wagons for the west coast market, and branch offices for wagon and carriage sales soon appeared in New York City,

Chicago, Atlanta, Kansas City, Omaha, Dallas, and many other cities. No other wagon manufacturer could equal the nationwide network of Studebaker sales locations.

When the Studebaker Brothers Manufacturing Company incorporated in 1868 it had assets of almost $250,000 and employed 190 men and boys. The entire capital stock of $75,000 was provided by Clement, John M., and Peter Studebaker, with no help from bankers or outside investors. The company grew steadily, rebuilding at once after a disastrous fire in 1874 which almost destroyed the factory. Jacob Studebaker joined his brothers on a full-time basis in 1875, and took charge of making carriages and buggies. That year the new factory produced vehicles worth more than $1,000,000 for the first time.

Studebaker was the largest employer in South Bend, with 240 workers in 1870 and 890 by 1880. Many of the men came from the growing stream of immigrants from Poland and Hungary. Although many other factories employed large numbers of young workers, fewer than ten per cent of Studebaker workers were boys, and there were only half a dozen women on the payroll in 1880. The basic Studebaker product was a farm wagon with a straight-sided grain box, usually painted dark green with the wheels and running gear in red and the name 'Studebaker' in yellow and red on the side of the box. But the company made a wide variety of vehicles, from army supply wagons and ambulances used in the Indian Wars to ice wagons for city delivery and paddywagons for the police force. There was a heavy freight wagon for hauling two tons of Nevada silver ore and a special light-weight one-horse model for Georgia cotton farmers. Studebaker also manufactured elegant carriages and workaday buggies. Benjamin Harrison, the only Hoosier ever elected to the White House, ordered three carriages and two mail buggies for the presidential stable in 1889. By the end of the century Studebaker advertised itself as the world's largest vehicle manufacturer, with an annual capacity of 75,000 vehicles and sales of more than $3,000,000. Both wagons and carriages were exported to countries as far away as South Africa, China, and Australia.

THE GREAT STUDEBAKER WAGON WORKS.

THE LARGEST IN THE WORLD.

Established in 1852 at South Bend, Ind.

FACILITIES SUFFICIENT TO MAKE A WAGON ON AN AVERAGE INSIDE OF 7 MINUTES.   200 HORSE POWER ENGINE.

C. STUDEBAKER, President.	P. E. STUDEBAKER, Treasurer.	WM. MACK, Cashier.
J. M. STUDEBAKER, Vice President.	J. F. STUDEBAKER, Secretary.	H. L. HINDS, Sup't Wagon Works.

The Studebaker Brothers' Wagon Works with a view of the ruins, the unburned buildings, the lumber shed after the fire 1874.

Immigration and the Great World War

Studebaker and South Bend grew up together. When Henry and Clement Studebaker opened their blacksmith shop in 1852 South Bend was a small town of about 1,700 people, joined to the world by a railroad which had arrived only a year earlier. By 1900 it was a bustling city of 36,000 residents, one out of every four born in a foreign country. Most of the immigrants in South Bend came from eastern Europe and, although in the old country they were chiefly farmers, most of them now made their living as factory workers. They worked at the Oliver plow works and the Singer sewing machine cabinet plant as well as Studebaker, for South Bend was never a one-company town. Nevertheless, Studebaker was the largest employer, and many hundreds of Polish and Hungarian workers lived in neighborhoods to the west and southwest of downtown South Bend, where their small but well-kept homes were located within the sound of the factory's steam whistle which called them to work early in the morning and signaled lunch time and the end of the ten-hour work day.

Many immigrants lived comfortably without ever learning English, because people in all the neighborhood shops and offices could speak the appropriate language, whether Polish on Western Avenue and West Washington Avenue or Hungarian on West Indiana Avenue. The children of the newcomers did learn English at school, whether a public school or at parish schools such as St. Hedwig or Our Lady of Hungary. Many sons followed their fathers into the bustling factories, while their daughters often worked in the clothing plants which were located in South Bend because there was an ample supply of female labor. The First World War and then legal restrictions slowed immigration to a trickle after 1914, but the census of 1920 showed that the booming city of South Bend had almost doubled its population in 20 years, to 71,000. Almost one out of every five residents was born outside the United States, and the proportion of immigrants among industrial workers was even greater.

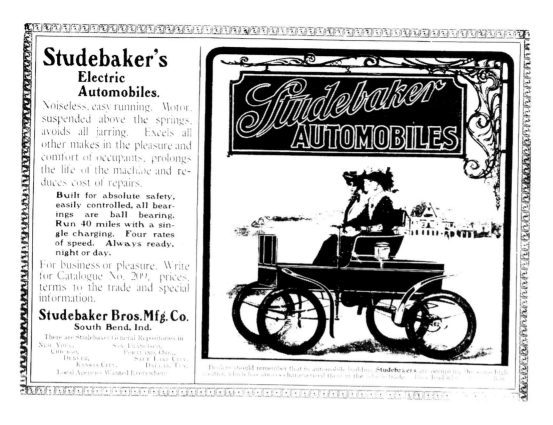

John M. Studebaker was the last of the five brothers and he continued as president of the company until 1911 when it was reorganized as the Studebaker Corporation and listed on the New York Stock Exchange. By that time it had become an important manufacturer of the new horseless carriages, beginning with an electric automobile in 1902 and expanding to gasoline-powered models two years later. Studebaker was the only carriage and wagon manufacturer among the 6,200 which were operating at the turn of the century to survive the transition to the automobile age. Except for the engine the early horseless carriages were much like buggies, with wooden frames, spoked wheels, upholstered seats, and sides and tops made from leather and waterproofed canvas. The same skilled workmen continued their daily work much as before, and it was years before the steel frame and sheet metal body became the standard for the automobile industry.

Studebaker Electric Piano Wagon

To Q/R Erskine   Thos Q Edison.

AT "STEERING LEVER" GEORGE MEISTER EDISON   MAN
PAYMASTER; AT HIS RIGHT, MR. EDISON

Thomas A. Edison bought the second electric car produced by Studebaker. Pictured at steering lever is George Meister, the Edison Company Paymaster; at his right, Mr. Edison.

The 1904 "Garford," the first gasoline powered vehicle manufactured by the Studebaker company.

Farm wagons remained an important segment of the business until 1920, but carriage and buggy sales declined rapidly after 1907 as the automobile captured the market among city residents. In 1908 Studebaker made a production and sales arrangement with Everett-Metzger-Flanders of Detroit and entered the auto business on a large scale. Everett-Metzger-Flanders came under complete Studebaker control the following year, but most of the company's automobile production remained in Detroit until the early 1920s. From 1911 onward the Studebaker Corportion was chiefly an automobile company, managed by John M.'s son-in-law, Frederick S. Fish. During the First World War Studebaker produced its last important orders of horse-drawn wagons, ambulances and gun mounts for the British, French, and then the American armies, as well as an enormous harness order for the British army.

14

Touch-up experts in high button shoes help camouflage 4.7 inch gun carriages which Studebaker turned out in volume during World War I.

Erskine, Bankruptcy and The Struggle Back

John Mohler Studebaker retired in 1915 and died two years later at the age of 83. Fred Fish became chairman of the board, and the dynamic salesman Albert R. Erskine took over as president. Erskine decided that the company should concentrate on automobiles and John M. Studebaker's last contribution to the company was persuading him to build the automobile works in South Bend rather than Detroit. Erskine sold off the farm wagon business and constructed a complex of large factory buildings where the wagon works and lumber yards had once stood. With few changes these buildings from the early 1920s served Studebaker until it decided to leave South Bend in 1963. Erskine took great pride in the company's good relations with its 7,000 workers, and Studebaker advertised its proud tradition of craftsmanship passed on from father to son. During the 1920s the company built several housing developments for its workers on the west side of South Bend, and began to provide paid vacations, a pension plan, and a special bonus paid on the anniversary of a worker's joining Studebaker. Erskine once boasted to a business magazine that "Our men build their very souls into the Studebaker cars."

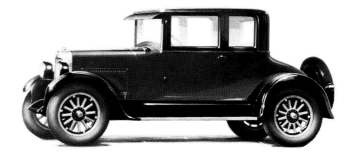

There were no labor troubles during these prosperous years, but Erskine surely exaggerated when he said that "Every man eats and thinks and dreams Studebaker." Albert Erskine certainly dreamed automobiles, and successful ones at that. In 1926 he introduced a new lighter model called the Erskine Six, and for several years it sold in fair numbers in France and Britain as well as the United States.

Knute Rockne, the famed Notre Dame football coach, was hired by Erskine in 1928 to inspire Studebaker salesmen with the same stirring style of locker room talks he used to rouse his players to so many gridiron victories. In March, 1931, Rockne was appointed manager of sales promotion activities with the possible intention of working full time for Studebaker when he retired from coaching at Notre Dame. Two weeks later he died in an airplane crash. In September Studebaker announced plans for a new low-priced car called the Rockne to be built in Detroit. Erskine mentioned that Knute Rockne would have been vice president of the Rockne Motors subsidiary had he lived, but this is not confirmed by other sources. The basic Rockne 65 was bargain priced at $585, but in the midst of the Depression there were few buyers. Production was shifted to South Bend in April, 1933, and closed permanently five months later.

Knute Rockne and Notre Dame football players pose with a Studebaker "Dictator Victoria," at Notre Dame Stadium in 1927.

Two of Studebaker's three management teams of its first 100 years are pictured at left. The team of Frederick Fish and A.R. Erskine; and the team of Harold Vance and Paul Hoffman.

BOARD OF DIRECTORS — THE STUDEBAKER CORPORATION — OCTOBER 31, 1927

FRONT ROW— *J. M. Studebaker, Jr.*   *John F. Harris*   *A. R. Erskine*   *Frederick S. Fish*   *Herbert H. Lehman*   *C. L. Bockus*   *James H. Perkins*
SECOND ROW—*H. S. Vance*   *Waddill Catchings*   *F. Studebaker Fish*   *Elmer T. Stevens*   *Edward N. Hurley*   *Frederick W. Longfellow*   *Paul G. Hoffman*

Albert R. Erskine was a proud figure among businessmen in a great era of American business, but unlike the solid Studebaker brothers he paid out large dividends rather than putting profits from the good years back into the business itself. His optimism was not diminished by the Wall Street Crash of 1929 and he continued to pay generous dividends an push new models. The Great Depression forced sales lower and lower. Although the company made a small profit, it paid a much larger dividend in 1931. The Studebaker Corporation reported its first loss the following year, and in March of 1933, just a few weeks after Franklin D. Roosevelt became president, the company went into receivership. Erskine was pushed into retirement and some weeks later shot himself.

Unlike so many other famous automobile manufacturers of the 1920s Studebaker did not disappear during the Depression. It was the only automobile company successfully reorganized under the bankruptcy laws, thanks to the exceptional efforts of a new leadership team. Paul Hoffman and Harold Vance had worked for Studebaker more than twenty years, and they knew the business and the company well. They understood the importance of continuing in production, especially when the situation was most desperate, in order to preserve the dealer network and to persuade both suppliers and customers that Studebaker was in business to stay. Hoffman telephoned the bankruptcy judge at one o'clock in the morning to ask permission to spend $100,000 of the firm's scarce supply of cash for a special advertising campaign. 'Studebaker Carries On," the nationwide advertisements read, and the South Bend factory resumed production under the authority of the bankruptcy court only three days after the company 'failed.' Hoffman and Vance used special dealer discounts to keep the dealers loyal to Studebaker and to turn the large inventory of unsold cars into much-needed cash. Of course the factory worked only two or three days a week during

the depths of the Depression, and Erskine's pension plan and anniversary bonuses were discontinued. Many workers were laid off, and wages were not as high as they had been during the prosperous years of the 1920s, but Studebaker survived and within two years emerged from bankruptcy as a going and successful business. With the help of their workers, Hoffman the master financier and salesman, and Vance, the expert production manager, achieved what many in the industry had thought impossible—they had saved Studebaker while such proud automotive names as Auburn, Marmon and Duesenberg vanished into memory.

Studebaker survived, but it was not the same as it had been and neither was the world in which it competed. The workers were not the same either, at least not in their way of thinking. Harold Vance was an old automobile production boss, and his door was open to any man from the assembly line who had a complaint, but working men were no longer willing to rely on the good will of a few company officers. They wanted protection from abusive foremen and they wanted a formal contract to spell out their rights. In other words they wanted a union. The National Industrial Recovery Act of 1933 offered federal encouragement for union organization as part of the New Deal's program for the revitalization of the American economy. Almost all of the existing unions were specialized groups of skilled workers organized by crafts within the loose structure of the American Federation of Labor. During June and July of 1933, 17 Studebaker workers joined together and became the charter members of a new union, Federal Labor Union No. 18310. The American Federation of Labor had no idea how to deal with large numbers of assembly line workers, and established unions representing machinists, electricians, millwrights and foundry molders argued that automobile workers should join the unions of their approprite crafts rather than a single industrial union. Wages were not an issue in 1933, when 25 per cent of all American workers were unemployed and many of the others were on short

1939 Studebaker Champion.

hours and reduced wages. What mattered was job security and working conditions, and the American Federation of Labor craft structure offered little to the less skilled workers of such industries as automobiles and steel.

Paul Hoffman and Harold Vance, struggling to reorganize the company under court supervision, did not actively oppose the union movement, and Studebaker workers faced none of the stern opposition which characterized General Motors or the violent oppression of Ford. FLU No. 18310 had as much difficulty with the American Federation of Labor as it did with management, and late in 1934 Studebaker was able to increase wages by five cents per hour. The next year in a Detroit meeting hall representatives from the Studebaker plant in South Bend formed the largest delegation at the convention which organized the United Automobile Workers of America. The Studebaker workers became UAW Local No. 5, and signed a formal contract with the company on May 21, 1937.

The contract provided for a plant-wide seniority system, systematic job classifications, vacation pay, a forty hour week and time-and-a-half for overtime. There were disagreements and arguments enough, but Studebaker maintained its proud record of never having a strike. Local No. 5 had more than 7,000 members, representing all Studebaker employees except those classified as management, receiving an average wage of about 90 cents per hour.

With Paul Hoffman's success in financial reorganization and confidence in good labor relations it was time for Harold Vance and the engineers and designers to devise a distinctive new model to restore Studebaker's standing in the market. The Champion was introduced in 1939 as Studebaker's return to the low price field, contested unsuccessfully years earlier with the Erskine and the Rockne. The Champion was an immediate success, offering lighter weight, good economy and attractive styling, and Studebaker's future seemed assured.

World War Two

Problems came soon enough, but this time in the form of a new world war which brought great opportunities as well as worry and trouble. Studebaker's long standing reputation in Europe brought truck orders from the French and the British, and as Americans went back to work to build defense products they could afford to buy new cars in greater numbers than any year since 1929. By October of 1940 Studebaker was beginning to feel the pressure of steel and machine tool shortages, and production of the 1941 models was limited by the available supplies rather than the weekly sales reports. Engineers were already at work on a new two-and-a-half ton heavy duty truck, and it went into limited production in 1941. The 1942 model cars appeared on schedule in the fall of 1941, but production was limited and halted completely on February 1, 1942. For the duration Studebaker would be manufacturing only for military requirements.

Building trucks was nothing new for Studebaker, although it had never been a major truck producer before the war. A large proportion of Studebaker trucks were sent to Russia under Lend-Lease, and one government official returned with a story that some Russians were so grateful that their name for trucks, any truck, was 'Studebaker.' This may not be quite true, but Joseph Stalin did send an official letter of thanks, and many thousands of Studebaker trucks hauled Russian troops and supplies through the terrible snow and mud of the eastern front and into the heart of Nazi Germany. By the end of the war, Studebaker had built 197,678 heavy trucks.

Studebaker's other war work involved entirely new products. In the push to expand American aviation to unprecedented production levels, it was necessary to build new factories to produce the needed planes and engines. Studebaker was chosen by the Army Air Corps to build airplane

engines, and a $50,000,000 plant with 21 acres of floor space was constructed by the Defense Plants Corporation on Chippewa Avenue on the far south side of South Bend for this purpose. Ground was broken in January of 1941, and by late 1942 the plant was in volume production of Curtis-Wright nine cylinder radial engines for Boeing B-17 heavy bombers. When the war in Europe ended in May, 1945, production was halted, after Studebaker had built 63,789 of the Cyclone engines for the Flying Fortresses. Each engine contained 8,000 parts which had to be assembled with great precision, Before shipment to the Boeing factories each engine was run for more than six hours in a test cell to check that it met all specifications. Studebaker had the opportunity to purchase the Chippewa Avenue plant at the end of the war, but Vance could see no use for the enormous building and allowed the opportunity to pass. During the Korean War Studebaker returned to the plant to build army trucks again, and, when the war ended in 1953, the company continued truck production there on government contracts. Today the plant is owned by the AM General Corporation, a subsidiary of General Dynamics, and is still used to manufacture heavy army trucks as well as small delivery vehicles for the U.S. Postal Service.

In addition to the army trucks the main Studebaker auto plant also designed and built a strange vehicle known as the Weasel, whose very existence was a secret for two years. The Weasel was an awkward and complex contraption whose great virtue was its ability to move uphill or down, through mud, sand, snow, water and even the volcanic ash of Iwo Jima. When other war orders were being reduced in mid-1945, the Weasel remained in full production because it was so useful in the island battles of the Pacific. When production ended just after the Japanese surrender Studebaker had turned out 15,124 Weasels, but it could not see any peacetime use for an all-terrain vehicle and made no effort to develop a civilian market. Studebaker employed more than 17,000 men and women in South Bend during World War II without any sort of labor difficulty. Although high wartime taxes limited profits, sales soared to new heights and the company was able to pay off all of its pre-war debts. Reconversion to civilian automobile production took several months, but, to all appearances, the Studebaker Corporation and its thousands of workers seemed to be well placed to share in post-war prosperity.

Illustrations from the Scrap Book sent in appreciation to the Studebaker Corporation from the Soviet Government showing the use of Studebaker transports by Russian troops during World War II. The top photo is captioned in Russian: "Forward to the West."

II.
World War 2
to Shut Down

LOREN PENNINGTON, PhD

The Legacy of Depression and War

The Studebaker Corporation entered the post-war world with what appeared to be significant advantages. War-time contracts had fattened the company's purse considerably. The management team of Paul Hoffman and Harold Vance, which had pulled the company out of bankruptcy was still intact, and labor relations the two created were considered a model for American industry. Also, Studebaker had a good international operation. Most important, the Raymond Loewy organization had been kept busy during the war creating a revolutionary body design that allowed Studebaker to be the first in the field with a completely new car. The new model was chiefly the work of designer Virgil Exner, and "the ghost in Exner's basement" would capture the imagination of the American public.

But all this was the surface; underneath there were potentially serious difficulties and might-have-beens. Pearl Harbor had cut short the company's resurgence in the automobile field, and, though Studebaker did make siginifacnt profits from its war contracts, much of that profit went back to the government in the form of heavy war-time taxes. More important, the war brought thousands of new workers into the South Bend plant and, by the time heavy increases in production in 1949-50 had brought the work force to more than 22,000, the majority of the workers were men who had never known the trials of the depression and who lacked the company loyalty of the older workers.

Labor decisions made during and immediately after the war contributed to the difficulties. Studebaker did not operate on a system of individual and group piecework as did the rest of the auto industry. Shortly after the war, it instituted a system of incentive pay for its indirect labor as well. As a result, Studebaker workers were able to average an hourly rate 22% above that of the industry until the piecework and incentive systems were abolished in 1954. The Studebaker labor problem was not merely that of high wages; it was also a matter of low productivity. The number of labor hours in a Studebaker car or truck was considerably above that of competition. For one month in 1956 (admittedly a horrible example) the hours in a Studebaker car ballooned to more than 200. It was not until 1959 that the hours per car were reduced to less than 80.

So, as Studebaker faced the post-war auto market, it was beset by costs considerably higher than the competition, and especially the Big Three. There were several possible solutions. One was to cut labor costs and improve labor efficiency. But this would mean a show-down with the local union and would result in significant losses of production, at least in the short run. Moreover, it would run counter to the company's traditional benevolent labor policy, a policy which was part and parcel of the company's advertising. A second possibility was to improve manufacturing efficiency. Considering the company's antiquated multi-story plants, this possibility was limited. A third possible solution was for the company simply to sell its cars

Raymond Lowey

Virgil Exner

at a higher price than the competition. With the great sellers' market in the immediate post-war years, this could be done. But when competition became intense it would be necessary to convince the buying public that they should pay more for a Studebaker car because it was worth more. There was one other possible solution, and it was the main road the company took until the mid 1950s: volume production. The economics of the automobile industry are such that if a company, even a small one, can keep its production above the breakeven point, each unit produced will bring an enormous profit. But if (as the experience of the late 70s and early 80s proves) a company's production falls below the breakeven point, its losses will mount in almost geometric ratio to the reduced production. So long as the post-war sellers' market held up, then volume production was the answer. But once the American automobile industry became truly competitive, it was no longer a question of the company's ability to produce cars, but its ability to sell them, and this would mean that the real pressure was on the Studebaker dealers. As the company increasingly recognized, the dealer organization was not equal to the task. Too many Studebaker dealers thought in terms of a high profit per unit, even if it meant limited sales, rather than a low profit per unit on a large number of sales. James Nance, president of the company from 1954 to 1956, once put the matter very well when he said, "the company's problem is that the dealers as a group have a lower breakeven point than the company does."

From World War II to The Korean War

Studebaker began its production of post-war civilian vehicles in May of 1945, when the commercial truck line got under way. By October Studebaker had completed all its war contracts, but strikes in the steel industry and at the transmission supplier severly limited automobile production until the end of the year. When the company shut down in March of 1946 to change over to its new post-war model, only 19,275 cars had been produced. Production on the new models was little better. Because of continued supplier strikes and the battle among the auto companies for short supplies of steel, it was September before there was significant volume. In October the company finally began to operate with a profit, but only because of its large production of high-profit trucks. The auto

operation, with its low volume, continued to lose money. At this point, the company decided to improve its position by raising prices, justifying the raise by arguing the superior quality of Studebaker cars. The company finished the year with worldwide sales of 119,275 units, 42,562 of them trucks. Even with this volume there was an operating loss of over eight million, though tax refunds allowed the company to show a slight profit.

The real upturn in Studebaker's fortunes came in 1947. By March the company had an eight-month backlog of orders, and metropolitan dealers were unable to guarantee delivery in less than a year. The only problem was how to increase output to meet the demand. As Vance put it at the time, Studebaker was in danger of losing a great opportunity. Unless there was a drastic increase in production, Studebaker could hope for no more than 4% of the market, and would remain a struggling independent. But if it could increase production to 6% of the market—300,000 units per year—it could expect the greatest profits in its history. A three-fold plan was gradually put into operation.

The first step was to acquire the necessary supplies of steel. To do this, the company purchased the Empire Steel Company at Mansfield, Ohio. The only difficulty with Empire was that it could not produce the types of steel necessary for auto operations, and its production had to be sent to rolling mills for conversion at a penalty of $93 per ton. But Empire did provide a stop-gap until the steel industry was able to increase production to meet the auto industry's needs. The second step was to build an assembly plant on the East coast to augment the production of South Bend, The Los Angeles plant, and planned Canadian operation at Hamilton. The East coast plan would have the added advantage of saving $50 per unit in transportation costs to the eastern market. The third step was a complete double-shifting of South Bend auto production. If all these operations could be carried out, Studebaker could produce a minimum of 30,000 units a month, and the volume would allow it to cut prices to more competitive levels.

As production built up, profits rose. In 1947, 191,000 units, including 68,000 trucks, produced an after-tax profit of nine million. In 1948, the company built 233,000 units and increased profits to 19 million. For the 1950 model run, the company introduced its aero nose, and the next year a new V-8 engine for its Commander line. For calendar year 1949, the company built 304,000 cars and trucks, and turned an after tax profit of $28,000,000. For the first time since the war, the company was able to cut prices. When the Board of Directors met on February 1, 1950, Vance told them that "the dealers are yelling for cars, and it looks as if we are going to be in a sold-out condition for several months to come." On May 1, 1950, the South Bend plant went to a full second shift and was churning out 1,160 cars a day. Los Angeles, Hamilton, and the declining but still substantial truck production added to the totals. Still it was not enough, and the company went forward with its plans for an assembly plant at New Brunswick, New Jersey, which would produce an additional 360 cars daily. In June, factory sales of cars and trucks reached 35,353, the highest in Studebaker history. Amidst all the optimism, no one noticed an event that would seriously

affect the company's fortunes. On Sunday, June 25, 1950, North Korean troops moved across the 38th parallel into South Korea, and the nation once again became embroiled in war.

To say that the Korean War was the only factor in Studebaker's changing situation would be an exaggeration. By September of 1950, factory sales were down to just over 30,000 units, and by November they were down to 23,000 and profits for that month were only a half million. In May of 1951, the company reduced the night shift and shelved its plans for production in the now completed New Brunswick plant. When the government imposed quotas on all auto manufacturers to conserve steel and other materials for war purposes, Vance expected that the company would still be able to produce all the cars it could sell. He was wrong. In August, car sales suddenly turned upward, dealer stocks fell to less than a month's supply, and the government restrictions began to pinch. To compensate for the declining volume of production, Studebaker asked for and received an exception to the government's price freeze. Higher prices would be the temporary and partial answer to decreased volume. Even so, with only 15% decline in production from 1950 to 1951 profits fell by nearly one-half. The decline in volume was beginning to take its toll.

Harold Vance stands beside the last car of Studebaker's first century of production.

Three generations of Studebaker workers pose with a "Commander" for this 1952 promotional photograph.

1953 "Champion" Hard Top

1953 Four Door Sedan

In 1952, the Studebaker Corporation celebrated its 100th year on the road. The aero nose was dropped for more conventional (though somewhat European) front end styling. Production declined another 15% to just under 232,000 vehicles. But dollar sales were up by 20%, and the company finished the year with a profit of more than 14 million. Vance and other company officials looked to the future with renewed optimism.

In June of 1952, production controls expired and, so it seemed, at a most favorable time. The company had spent $27,000,000 to ready its second all-new post-war car. The new European look sport coupes and hardtops designed by Bob Bourke of the Raymond Loewy organization became one of the great aesthetic triumphs in American automobile history. But the sedans on which the coupe and hardtop styling were grafted were considered by many (to put it kindly) ugly. Further, the 1953 models marked the beginning of a problem that plagued the corporation for the rest of its automotive career: rapid and persistent body rust that seriously diminished the company's claim that it produced a quality automobile.

There was yet another problem on the 53 models: they proved to be a production nightmare. It was not until April that sufficient volume was obtained to put the auto operations in the black for the model year. Almost immediately disaster struck in another form. In May, the workers at the Warner Gear Division of Borg-Warner Corporation went out on a prolonged strike in which each side refused to give an inch. The strike left Studebaker without a standard transmission supplier and, at the end of that month, the company was forced to shut down Canadian and truck operations and put Los Angeles and South Bend on half time until the end of the strike allowed the resumption of full production in July.

Worse was yet to come. In the fall of 1953 Ford and Chevrolet began an all-out production race, the retail market became completely disorganized, and dealers of all makes were offering large discounts and overallowances on trade-ins. Paul Hoffman, who had left the company in 1948 to head European Recovery and had only recently returned as part-time President, remarked that the market was the most disorganized he had seen it in his 42 years in the business. Vance told the Board that dealer morale was the lowest in the company's history, and that no profit could be expected for the rest of the year. Production on 54s, which began in October at less than 900 cars per day in all plants, was shut down for two weeks in December, and resumed in January on a four day week. The high hopes for 1953 ended with a profit of less than three million dollars, none of which came from car production.

In the first quarter of 1954, the company lost more than it had made in the entire previous year, and rumors were abroad that Studebaker was about to collapse. By April, the company officials concluded that they would have to reduce the price of their car, and the only way to do it was to get rid of the 22% premium Studebaker workers were able to make through the piecework system. It was announced that Paul Hoffman was returning to the company full-time for a hundred days to ramrod an effort to get rid of the piecework system and replace it with measured day rate. Hoffman had his work cut out for him, but with the help of the workers, he succeeded. From now on Studebaker hourly wages would be competitive. But the problem was not only wage rates, it was also standards. Under the piecework system, standards, low though they were, were self-enforcing because the individual worker or his group lost money if they were not met. But with the new day rate system, there was no penalty for not making production and, from then on, it was up to Studebaker's foreman system to enforce and increase production standards. For this task the Studebaker foreman was completely unprepared, and it would be another five years before competitive work standards were achieved.

During the months the new union agreement was being negotiated, Studebaker continued to lose money in ever increasing amounts. The five million dollar operating loss of the first quarter of 1954 jumped to twelve million in the second. More would have to be done if the company was to be saved. Company management now began to look with increasing interest on a possibility they had previously rejected: merger with another automobile company.

The Packard and Curtis-Wright Years

The best prospect for merger was the Packard Motor Car Company. Like Studebaker, Packard was an old-line company with a substantial reputation. But by 1951, Packard was losing money, and its directors realized that,if the company was to continue in the auto business, vast changes would have to be made in its operations. As the man to effect these changes, the directors selected James J. Nance of Hotpoint, and Nance took over in March of 1952. By 1953, Nance decided that Packard would have to have more modern production facilities.

Paul G. Hoffman

Photo Courtesy: *The South Bend Tribune*

James J. Nance

His first step was the conversion of the Packard defense plant at Utica, Michigan, to automated production of V-8 engines and transmissions. The second was to move assembly operations from the antiquated Boulevard Plant to the Conner Plant, which was leased from Chrysler. There Packard could not only assemble cars, but for the first time since 1941 build its own bodies. The net cost of these two moves was over forty million dollars, a sum that could be recovered only if Packard volume could be increased beyond what might reasonably be expected. So like Studebaker Packard was faced, though for very different reasons, with the prospect of operating well below its breakeven point. The solution seemed to be a merger with another auto company whose product was in a lower-priced line so that the merged company could effect the supposed savings of a full-line company. The banks and insurance companies

were enamored with the idea, and were willing to make a total of 70 million in credit available to the merged company. This was perhaps the most important reason why Studebaker, which had previously rejected Packard overtures, was willing· to go along.

The union of Studebaker and Packard into the new Studebaker-Packard Corporation was not exactly a merger. Because of possible troubles with stockholders, it was deemed more expedient for Packard to take over Studebaker. The takeover was completely friendly. Nance became President of the new company and Chief Operating Officer, Hoffman became Chairman of the Board, and Vance headed the Executive Committee. In practice, Nance would run the corporation, to the great resentment of the Studebaker people, who would refer to the years 1954-56 as the 'Packard Operation.' At the time of the takeover in October of 1954, Nance calculated that the new company would lose an acceptable nine million dollars in 1955, reduce that to a small loss in 1956, and make a considerable profit on its integrated models in 1957 and 1958. But very quickly these assumptions broke down because of mistaken calculations of the breakeven point for each car line. At the time of merger negotiations Packard's breakeven had been set at 64,000 cars per year and Studebaker's at 165,000 cars and trucks annually. The estimates were both far too low. Studebaker actually managed 138,000 units of the 1955 model, only 27,000 below estimate, but lost $15,000,000. Packard produced 62,000 cars, only two thousand below the supposed breakeven point, but because of continual production problems which led to off-standard labor costs at the Conner Plant and the terrible quality of the 55 Packard, Packard lost $15,000,000 as well.

Despite the unexpected 30 million dollar loss in 1955, the situation was by no means hopeless. However, the future depended on a number of unpredictable factors: (1) Would industry-wide car production for 1956 at least approach the record level of 7.8 million cars? The answer was no. (2) Could Packard, with its slightly facelifted 1956 model, maintain its share of whatever 1956 market there was? Again, the answer was no. (3) Could the drasticaly restyled 1956 Studebaker, which had

The Packard Clipper

dropped the foreign look for more conventional styling, increase its share of the market? Again no. (4) Could Nance and his colleagues raise the fifty million dollars in additional capital they needed— twenty million to strengthen the sagging dealer organization and thirty million for the new 1957 Packard? The answer to this was a very decided no. The banks and insurance companies had concluded that further investment was useless and that the time had come to bail out.

Beginning in late January of 1956, the Board of Directors set up a finance committee under director J. Russell Forgan. It investigated every possible avenue: a loan from the Federal Reserve Bank of New York, or even from the Big Three; new large defense contracts; mergers with a number of companies both inside and outside the auto industry; and sale of some of the company's plants. When everything failed, the directors considered liquidation, but concluded that this would lead to a total 'washout' for the stockholders. A solution was finally reached by the most roundabout methods. Hoffman was a close friend of President Eisenhower and, because of this and other reasons, Ike decided that Studebaker-Packard could not be allowed to fail. Treasury Secretary George Humphrey was put in charge of the details. From April until August it was touch and go, but a very complex deal was finally worked out. The Curtis-Wright Corporation entered into an agreement to provide management help for Studebaker, and in return received an option to buy five million shares of unissued Studebaker-Packard common stock at five dollars per share, an option which, if exercised, would give Curtis-Wright control of the company. All Studebaker-Packard defense contracts and the Utica and Chippewa plants were turned over to Curtis-Wright in return for a payment of $35 million. An additional ten million dollars was put into the till by Daimler-Benz AG of Stuttgart, Germany, manufacturers of the prestigious Mercedes-Benz, in return for which Studebaker would distribute the cars of DBAG in North America. All of Studebaker-Packard's American operations were concentrated at the South Bend Main. With the 45 million dollars from the deal, and the postponement of debt obligations by its creditors, Studebaker continued on the rocky road of American automobile production for the next seven years.

Interlude

Nance, Hoffman, and Vance were now gone from the scene, and leadership of the reorganized corporation fell to the new president, Harold E. Churchill, a homespun type who farmed as a hobby. Churchill was a distinct contrast to the flamboyant Nance and Hoffman. Churchill created a management team of A.J. Porta as Vice-President and Finance Officer, C.M. MacMillan as Director of Industrial Relations, and Sidney Skillman as head of sales, and set about the task of restoring the company's auto operations under the direction of Curtis-Wright and its president, Roy Hurley.

Harold E. Churchill

Nance, like his predecessors, had thought in terms of volume production. Hurley thought in terms of cost-cutting. But in spite of the difference in philosophy, Hurley would not be more successful than Nance. No matter how much costs were cut, a certain volume had to be achieved.

Successes on the 1957 model were small. To mollify the Packard dealers who otherwise would have nothing to sell, Churchill, for a million dollars, managed to cobble together a Packard on a Studebaker chassis with Packard front and rearend styling. It was soon dubbed the 'Packabaker'. It was never much of a seller, and was dropped after 1958. The company also tried to compete with the lower priced Chevrolets and Fords by introducing the 'Scotsman', a stripped-down Champion with the cheapest possible trim. It sold well in both 1957 and 1958, but it was a low-profit item and, after studying the sales reports, Porta concluded that it was not really competing with other makes—it was competing with more profitable Studebakers. It, too, was dropped after 1958.

Throughout 1957, there was no improvement in the company's profit picture, but Churchill and Porta hoped to turn the company around in the last quarter of the year with the facelifted but flashier 58 models, and to hold the loss for the year to some four million.

During 1956 and 1957 Studebaker had managed at last to get labor hours down to under a hundred per car, and the breakeven point stood at 130,000 units. Porta was hoping for sales of 162,000 on the 58 model, including Mercedes-Benz models and 12,000 of the 'Goggomobile', a small German car for which the company had great hopes. With that volume, the expected profit was ten million. None of this came to fruition. The Goggomobile was a total flop and was never marketed, Mercedes-Benz sales were held back by the refusal of DBAG to provide anywhere near enough cars for potential sales, and die failures put the company more than a month behind in its production of 58 Studebakers, and the company continued to lose dealers. By November Porta estimated that Studebaker might sell as few as 80,000 units on its 58 model, and would again lose money, perhaps as much as twelve million. Hurley was irate at the adverse turn of events, and told the Board that the company would be out of cash by January and 'the jig will be up.' The bank let it be known that they would not take another merger like the Packard fiasco. There was only one ray of hope. In December of 1957 Churchill told the Board that he had a new idea for the 59 models, but he was not yet ready to present it. In January, the Board discussed going into bankruptcy, but Churchill persuaded them to hold off until they saw the new car in February. His plan was for a new small sedan on a 108.5 wheelbase, and a continuation of the Hawk. The cost would be only 7.3 million, and a profit could be expected on a mere 115,000 units.

By mid-1958, the two-fold Studebaker game plan was in place: (1) Build the new small car, and (2) Pursue a vigorous acquisition policy, which,

even if the auto operations failed, would allow Studebaker to remain in business. To carry out the latter, A.M. Sonnabend of Botany Mills and a master of merger was brought on to the Board. Hurley decided to withdraw Curtis-Wright from the operation, and declined to exercise the stock option. The creditors agreed to delay the payment of part of the Studebaker debt, and to exchange the rest for equity in the form of convertible preferred stock, on the basis of one share of convertible preferred for each $233 of debt. At conversion time, each share of convertible could be converted to 33 shares of common. The bottom line was that if Studebaker common was selling for at least $7 per share at conversion time, the creditor would recover all the money they had put into equity. As it turned out, they made a substantial profit.

Up With The Lark

By October, 1958, the new car, now named the Lark, was under production. It had already been shown to the dealers, and for once they were ecstatic. 278 new dealers had been signed since June, and the company had 30,000 orders in hand. South Bend Main was on overtime at 54 cars per hour. Things were going so well that Churchill and Porta had to hold the directors back—it would be

February, they said, before they knew if they were out of the woods. Churchill and Porta could hardly believe what followed. By introduction day on November 14, the plant was on a 53 hour week, and on November 14, production was increased to 60 per hour. New dealers were flocking in, and there was even talk of restoring the second shift and of putting Studebaker auto operations into a new plant. Churchill and Porta opposed this last suggestion—they never believed a one story plant had all the operating efficiencies that some claimed. After a three day strike late in the month, a new labor agreement was worked out that for once was slightly under the industry standard. As of December 10th, the company had received more than 65,000 dealer orders, as compared to 44,000 on the entire 58 model. On December 29th, the line speed was increased to 70 per hour, and the 53 hour work week remained in effect. Skillman wanted a second shift, but Churchill held him back. Instead, he pushed production to 84 cars per hour, the highest in the company's history. The profit for the first half of 1959 was more than eleven million, and it was all tax-free.

The sudden prosperity brought a new problem. It was the second part of the Studebaker plan: the acquisitions policy. The question was where to put the profits, and it was over this question that the unity of the Board began to break down. One group, led by Porta, argued for putting them into the auto operation, especially as it now promised to produce enough profits to allow Studebaker to recover nearly all its tax credits. Sonnabend argued that the future of the company demanded diversification. Even the members of the Board who did not line up with either side found his proposed mergers with such companies as Manhattan Shirt, Magnus Organ, and Revlon 'undignified' for a company of Studebaker's reputation, and Sonnabend found himself increasingly frustrated. A small third faction, headed by New York investment banker Frank Manheim, was completely opposed to Sonnabend, but tended to put Mercedes-Benz operations first in their thinking, sometimes to the detriment of Studebaker. A fourth opinion was added when Studebaker acquired Gravely

Tractor and brought its President, D. Ray Hall, onto the Board. Hall was a volatile character who thought he was the only one who could save the company. Eventually, he would cause even more trouble than Sonnabend. For the moment, the proponents of Studebaker automobile operations held the field, but even they recognized that 1960, when the Big Three were scheduled to enter the compact field, might be a different ball game.

At the time the Lark was under consideration, the plan was to facelift in 1960 and 1961, and to bring out another car for the 1962 model. As the 1960 model year began to develop, it appeared at first that the Big Three entrance into the compact field would not appreciably affect Lark sales. By September of 1959, the company had more than 38,000 orders in hand, 10,000 above the previous year. Porta had been promoted to head the auto operation, and Byers Burlingame, who had distinguished himself in the Packard close-out, had become the company's chief financial officer. At the September director's meeting, Burlingame presented his current report and plans for the future. With his usual caution, he predicted the profit for the 1959 calendar year would reach 21 million (it would actually reach more than 28 million, and as Studebaker paid no income tax for the year, it was the highest after-tax profit in the company's history). Burlingame argued further that if the company did come out with a new car in 1962 at a cost of 36.5 million, profits over the three-year run of the model would amount to 63 million. But if the company had to drop the new model for a series of facelifts, which would cost only six million less than a new car, it could expect a six million dollar loss for the same period. The decision, he announced would have to be made 'today' so that tooling could commence in December. Studebaker was at the crossroads: should the company gamble on a new car, or should it spend its money on acquisitions, even if it meant the end of auto operations? The debate was long and difficult, but in the end Burlingame and Porta prevailed and the new car was authorized.

With this decision out of the way, the company concentrated on its 1960 production, still at 84 vehicles per hour. For a time, sales held up, but the competition of the Big Three proved increasingly strong, and in spite of short production weeks, by February sales were well behind production. The directors looked at the 1961 facelift and were disappointed in the extreme; even the all-new 1962 did not look like enough of a change. They decided to call in Raymond Loewy, and reconsider their 62 model plans.

By April the company was losing money. The directors considered dropping the all-new 1962 in favor of a facelift, and the wind-up of auto operations after the 1963 model. Sidney Skillman was let go as sales manager and replaced by Lou Minkle. At the June meeting, Burlingame told the Board the company would be lucky to break even in 1960, and Porta reported that Minkle had found the Studebaker dealer organization deplorable. Most of the dealers added in the last two years were duals with Big Three dealers, and the Big Three were putting pressure on them to drop the Lark line. Russell Forgan exploded, "Why have we been continually told that the dealer organization is improving, when we are now told that it is terrible?" The auto men had no real answer.

During the summer of 1960 the acquisitions policy went forward with the purchase of Clarke Floor Machine Company and Onan Generator, which with the already acquired Gravely Tractor, Gering Plastics, and Cincinnati Testing Laboratory, brought the acquisitions to five. None of them were the result of Sonnabend's work. In September, Churchill was replaced as Chief Operating Officer by Clarence Francis, though Churchill retained the office of President. Francis also became Chairman. In spite of falling sales the Board decided to continue with the new 1962 model.

Less than two months later, sales had declined still further and the company was facing disaster. At a special Board meeting on November 27, 1960, in the light of falling sales, a 'horror' as Manheim called them, the management of the auto operations confronted the Board with four alternatives.

"South Bend Main"

The first was liquidation of the auto operations in April of 1961; the second and third were for major and minor facelifts on the 1962 model; and the last was for the all new 1962, including a new four cylinder engine. The Board was aghast, especially as it became plain that management, after arguing so long for the new car, now favored a facelift. Minkle claimed that he could sell a facelift to the dealers and improve the dealer organization if he could also promise them a four cylinder engine in the future. The Board looked at the cost of liquidation—55 million dollars—and decided to go along with the major 3.5 million facelife, even though it appeared to mean abandoning any real prospects for the future of auto operation.

The December meeting of the Executive Committee was equally stormy, but for a different reason. Francis began by announcing that Sonnabend was ready to quit. He also announced that he had offered the position of President and Chief Operating Office to Sherwood Egbert of McCulloch Chain Saw. Hall was absolutely opposed and demanded that he be given the job. Burlingame and Porta argued that Egbert was the only man who could turn the dealer organization around. The decision was put off until the full Board could meet on December 19th. By the time the Board met, Egbert had withdrawn as a candidate. Hall announced that he was ready to take over as head of

Studebaker Proving Grounds located west of South Bend. The name "Studebaker" is spelled out in 200 foot evergreen trees. It is reputed to be the largest, man-made, living monument in the world.

the company, and if chosen would embark on a program to save the auto operations by cutting costs and would oppose any further diversification. Sonnabend thereupon announced that he, too, was a candidate, and if elected he would pursue a vigorous acquisitions policy. But he was not for abandoning autos; he would put either Churchill or Porta in charge and give the man selected dictatorial powers. Churchill and Porta, surprised and pleased at Sonnabend's defense of the auto operations, supported Sonnabend. Manheim and Forgan led the pro-Hall forces. It was moved and seconded that Sonnabend be elected Chief Operating Officer, but at the last moment, the decision was again put off until the next meeting on December 28th.

When the directors reconvened on the 28th, Burlingame led off with his financial report that he had not been able to give the previous week. In the interim the situation had become even worse. There had been another fall-off in orders, and of the 560 cars built in the previous two days, only 200 were for dealers, and 360 went into factory stocks. "This situation," Porta said in conclusion, "Must be turned around in the next thirty days or the answer will be made for us in the next three or four months." For 1961 he was now predicting only 60,000 domestic units—almost as bad as 1958—and a 28 million dollar loss for the Auto Division. In Porta's view the company was down to two alternatives: a very minor facelife for 1962, or liquidation of the domestic auto business. Sonnabend argued that immediate heroic action was needed, and that action was himself as Chief Operating Officer. Hall again offered his own candidacy. Both men were excused from the meeting while the rest of the directors considered the claims of each. To add to the confusion Francis announced that Egbert had reconsidered and was willing to take the job. Churchill and Porta, miffed at Egbert's off-again on-again attitude, refused to support his election, and Sonnabend and Hall would not support him either. Francis did not believe that with four directors against him, Egbert would accept. Under the circumstances, Francis proposed that Churchill again be reinstalled as Chief Operating Officer.

Churchill flatly refused. Finally, almost without hope, Francis went off to telephone Egbert that Hall and Sonnabend were unalterably opposed to his election, and that the best that could be expected from Porta and Churchill was that they would abstain from actually voting against him. To his great surprise, Egbert answered in two words: "Let's go." Elated, Francis returned to the meeting and announced that he recommended Egbert be elected President and Chief Operating Officer and that he himself remain as Chairman. Sonnabend lost his temper. "This company is doomed," he said. "The decision is ridiculous. The Board should disband, get out. It is worthless". The vote on Egbert was taken; eight directors voted for him, Hall and Sonnabend against, and Porta and Churchill abstained.

The Rise and Fall of Sherwood Egbert

A week later on January 4, 1961, the Executive Committee met with Egbert present. It accepted Sonnabend's resignation. Egbert took immediate control; he himself would replace Sonnabend on the Executive Committee, and Hall was excluded from that policy making group. Each member pledged his support, but Porta remarked that he hoped Egbert would not confuse his quarterback job with that of cheerleader.

When the full Board met early in February, Egbert announced that Raymond Loewy had been retained to effect the 62 and 63 facelifts, but Loewy would have to work under Styling Director Randall Faurot—'we will make styling decisions, not Loewy.' What Egbert was doing was serving notice that he would be the dictator of auto operations. But there was still a question of the 1962 models—that was to be decided at the Board's meeting in March. Egbert did not wait that long. At another Board meeting later in February he proposed facelifts for 1962 and 1963, and an all new car for 1964 that would cost 35 to 40 million dollars to tool. The facelifted 62 models were shown, and the directors were extremely pleased—they did not believe they could get so much change for so little

Sherwood Egbert with the Avanti. The Avanti, with its styling surprisingly unchanged, is still being produced in South Bend more than twenty years later.

money. When Egbert asked for approval of his program for the next three years, even Hall went along. Finally Egbert announced, almost in passing, that he was planning an all-new fiberglass sports-car. It would become the Avanti.

The directors met again at the end of March and found that the unpredictable swings of the auto market had suddenly turned in Studebaker's favor. Dealer orders were up 33% over the previous month; the buying public was giving Egbert a vote of confidence. Egbert announced that the 62 models would start at a respectable 62 per hour, and once again would include the Hawk. At the same time, work was proceeding on the fiberglass sports car.

By April, sales had increased even further, and Burlingame predicted that Studebaker would finish the year with a loss of only 10 million, and would still have 25 million in cash. The fiberglass car X would be ready by the following April. By that May, the situation had reached the point where Egbert was able to announce that Studebaker had sold out the entire 1961 model run, and would have to delay the opening of ten new company dealerships in metropolitan areas because no cars were available. Further, DBAG had at last agreed to give Studebaker all the Mercedes-Benz cars it could sell. But in the midst of the new hopes, trouble was again brewing. D. Ray Hall had written the Board members an irate letter charging that Egbert was acting in a dictatorial fashion, and was not referring important

The Grand Tourismo Hawk

matters to the Board. The Board recognized that whatever Egbert was doing it seemed to be working, and Director Edward Litchfield moved a seven-part resolution in support of Egbert. Hall charged, 'this company is on the verge of bankruptcy,' and Egbert countered, 'If we ran it the way you want it run, it would be bankrupt.' Litchfield's motion passed with only Hall opposing.

By June the sales situation had improved still further and Egbert predicted a four million profit for 1962. When the Board met in July they were faced with a new and unexpected problem: Egbert had just undergone surgery for cancer. Along with this unhappy news, Hall dropped another bombshell. He had gotten together with his old enemy Sonnabend and had worked out a tentative plan with the Murcheson Brothers of the Allegheny Corporation, one of the nation's largest holding companies, for the purchase of a large block of Studebaker common. He made it clear that he intended to get control of the Board and get rid of Manheim, Litchfield, and Francis. By the next month Forgan had checked into Hall's claims, and found that the Murchesons had no real interest in Studebaker. Churchill, who at best had been lukewarm on Egbert, jumped into the fray, remarking that Egbert 'had done a hell of a job in South

Bend,' and the time had come to put an end to bickering and give Egbert the Board's full support. If Hall had ever had any real influence on the Board, it was now at an end.

In November, Burlingame reported that the company had a 'bang-up September.' The Hawk was doing especially well, and the company was planning to produce 10,000 of them on the 62 model. The new 64 models had been shown in Europe in two versions, one designed by Brooks Stevens, the other by Loewy; the Loewy version had been preferred. Plans were made to sell off Gering Plastics and CTL for more than 20 million dollars to raise funds to produce the new cars, and the other 20 million necessary were to be borrowed. But amidst the optimism there were the usual clouds. Another steel strike was in the offing, and the company was forced to stockpile steel as a hedge. It was time to reopen negotiations with the union, and according to MacMillan, the union demands amounted to more than eleven million, while the company was arguing for a small reduction. The Mercedes-Benz operation was again in trouble; the quality of the new Mercedes-Benz cars was terrible, and the company's second largest Mercedes-

Benz dealer had just quit. But when the Board discussed the auto situation at the end of the month, they decided to go forward with the new Loewy car. The only question was whether to make the big plunge on the 63 models, or wait until the 64s. They decided on caution. The fiberglass car would give them something new for 63, and a good facelift on the regular models would at last get rid of the troublesome dog-leg door pillar—and on the 64s, 'everything will be new from the tires up.'

By December, the company was getting ready for the one thing they usually tried to avoid—a major strike. Management had decided that, in spite of the competitive wage rates and work standards, there were still areas where the company was paying above the industry average. The chief item was personal time. Since 1942, Studebaker workers had been allowed 39 minutes of personal time per eight hour day. At Ford and GM, the amount was 24 minutes. The difference was 15 minutes of wash-up time: the Studebaker lines shut down five minutes early at lunch and ten minutes early at the end of the shift. Studebaker calculated that the wage bill for this fifteen minutes of lost production had, since 1942, cost the corporation $30,000,000. The comparison to GM and Ford was not entirely valid. At that time Chrysler was giving workers 37 minutes, AMC 40 minutes, and the workers at the Studebaker Hamilton plant, supposedly noted for its efficiency, were receiving a whopping 61 minutes per day. As the company prepared for the possible strike, it received encouraging news. The profit for the last quarter had reached 8.5 million, over three-fourths of which had come from the Auto Division, and, through a five million profit from the sale of Gering, it had managed a 2.5 million profit for the entire year.

In January, 1962, the strike hit. There were a number of bitter incidents, including the famous one in which, supposedly, Egbert and a worker came to blows. By the end of the month the profit for the previous year had been wiped out, and the losses continued into February. The settlement cost the company $.16 per hour in cost of living ajustment (COLA). As for the wash-up time that had been the chief issue, the company got back only five of the fifteen minutes.

Egbert turned his attention to acquisitions. Over the next several months there were three: Chemical Compounds, which produced the STP engine additive, Schaefer, a manufacturer of commercial refrigerators, and Andy Granatelli's Paxton Products, which produced a supercharger (though it was not really that) that was considered necessary for the fiberglass X car (now redubbed the RQ). Egbert was hoping for 7,500 of the RQ cars by September, and production of the 1963 Lark was set to begin on August 27th at 80 per hour (later reduced to 70). As car sales were running 25% above the previous year, this did not seem unduly optimistic, especially, as Egbert pointed out, since they had achieved this increase with 500 fewer dealers. And that was the rub: after all the effort that had been expended, the company had only 2,000 dealers. Egbert had already hinted to the Board that unless this number could be brought up to 2,400 by September, he had doubts as to whether they should spend the money to bring out the new 1964 model. However, soon Egbert came to the conclusion that the dealer organization could not be built up without a new car. Maybe the new Avanti would start the ball rolling.

Avanti production was in trouble from the beginning. The fiberglass parts were far off standard and, what was worse, they could not (as metal parts could) be made to fit by a little judicious hammering or bending. The 7,500 Avantis by August of 1962 never materialized. In June, production was only two cars per day; in July, Egbert described Avanti production as 'organized chaos.' By September, daily production was still only at ten. Even when reasonable production was at last achieved, the car did not sell.

Along with the Avanti difficulties, the acquisition program began to falter. By late 1962, plans were ready for the takeover of Trans-Internaional Airlines and Franklin Manufacturing Company. Trans-International was a complete failure. The Franklin acquisition cost Studebaker $41 million— $25 million of which was borrowed from six banks (thereby lessening Studebaker's chances for borrowing the cash to finance the new 64 models) and they soon ran into efficiency and sales problems. The 1963 model was having launch troubles, and Auto Division losses were again nearing the two

million a month level. By early November dealer orders were at 300-350 a day, nowhere near enough to sustain the seventy per hour rate. The minutes of an informal meeting of the Executive Committee held on the 2nd of November reported in an off-hand way 'December 7th Board meeting—will review 64 model... about $7 million tooling plus $4 million for 65 models.'

On the face of it, it looked as if the new 1964 model had been shelved. This was not true. On December 7th Egbert set forth an elaborate plan to superimpose a new Avanti II line over a continuing facelifted Lark line. The new Avanti would be ready in February of 1964, and would include the sports car and two and four door sedans, with a staton wagon to be added later. The total tooling bill for both 1964 lines would be 18.5 million, and another 11 million would be spent in 1965, part of it

on a new modular truck. The Lark would end with the 1966 model. The Board voted two million for 1964 Lark tooling, but, apparently at the instigation of Egbert, nothing for the Avanti II.

Plans for the auto operation now became increasingly intertwined with acquisitions policy. It was clear that auto profits, if any, could not begin to use up the company's tax credits and that further acquisitions would be required. Forgan had made a thorough survey of possibilities and had come up completely dry. The only immediate purchase was Domowatt, an Italian maker of electrical appliances. Soon after it was acquired, Domowatt was on the verge of bankruptcy. It was the third straight Egbert acquisition failure, a string of defeats that eventually added to Egbert's lack of credibility with the Board.

Two weeks after Egbert had presented his plan for the elaborate two-line 1964 models, the Board began to have some second thoughts. The Egbert proposal was based on the idea that Studebaker would produce 121,000 domestic cars on the 1963 model. What would happen if this was not achieved? As Forgan put it, 'would we bleed to death?' Francis suggested that they evaluate an alternative, Plan X, as he called it. Though the nature of Plan X was carefully concealed in the minutes for the next several months, it was a plan for liquidating auto operation.

In early January of 1963, the Board met for a session that went on for two days. Egbert proposed a total of six possible alternatives; eventually the Board came down to two: Plan A and Plan B. Plan A was for the two car lines for 1964. Plan B was for liquidation of the auto business. The Board voted 7 to 2 for Plan A, with Hall and Forgan opposed, Forgan because he did not think the banks would agree to finance the two models, especially as they had already lent the money for the purchase of Franklin. By March, it was clear that the banks would not advance the money for the new Avanti II portion of Plan A unless the company would put up the acquired divisions as security. In light of the falling sales on the 1963 model, Egbert thought this too much of a risk, and recommended that the 1964 line be cut back to the facelifted Lark. As in the case of the proposal for a new 1962 line, inability to secure financing and fears that the dealer organization was too weak to bring the necessary sales had brought an end to plans for a new car. But management went ahead with plans to start the 64 Larks at 60 per hour, which would produce 43,000 by the end of the year. By December it was expected that they would have an idea as to the sales success of the 64 model. If it did not succeed, Plan B was ready.

In June, Francis stepped down as Board Chairman and was replaced by Randolph Guthrie. When the Board met in August, Guthrie presented his view of the situation. It was a bleak but accurate history of the company's last ten years. He pointed out that since 1953 the company had lost money in automobile production every year except 1959. The company had not had the money to bring out new models or to modernize the plant, and in spite of continuous efforts to bolster it, without new models the dealer organization had deteriorated. Because of inability to secure financing for the two-line 64 plans, the model had become just another facelift. The chances for securing money for a new model in the future were slim, particularly in the face of the Avanti's sales failure. At any rate, it was now almost too late to retool for a completely new 65 model. Guthrie still hoped the 64 model might succeed, but he was not optimistic. If it did not succeed, the company had three alternatives: Struggle along with the Auto Division in the hope things would improve and offset auto operations with the profits from the acquired divisions, cut automobile operations drastically (apparently by ending production at South Bend), or put Plan B into operation. Egbert spoke next. He did not think the future of auto operations as bleak as Guthrie had painted it; the 1964 Lark had a practically new body, while Guthrie was going on 1963 model experience. Egbert thought a better comparison was 1961 when, with a minor facelift, the company had done reasonably well. Forgan found the comparison with 1961 invalid—the company owed a lot more money now (the result, chiefly, of the Franklin acquisition). And now Forgan came to the heart of the matter: 'On the other hand, prospects now of continuing the Company without the Auto Division are brighter than they were in 1961.' For the first time the company could end automobile production and remain in business. The Board agreed to go ahead with the 1964 model, but to limit supplier committments and reassess the situation every two weeks.

When the Board met on September 25th, Egbert reported that the banks were willing to stretch out the payments on the 25 million borrowed to acquire Franklin, but they would not put a dime into the auto business, nor would they allow the profits from the acquired divisions to be used for auto operations. Unless the 1964 model succeeded, the bank decision would be the last nail in the coffin for automotive operations in South Bend. The 64 model introduction was set for the next day. The model failed completely. By late October production was cut to 35 an hour and 2,450 employees were laid off.

1964 Lark Daytona

The Board met on November 1, heard the dreary news, and that afternoon went into an unrecorded executive session. When it returned to regular session, Guthrie instructed the secretary to record that the executive session had been 'on the subject of policy disagreements with the President.' While it cannot be confirmed, Egbert apparently insisted on the continuance of auto operations at South Bend. Guthrie further announced that as Egbert was scheduled for more surgery the next week, he had been put on indefinite leave. Byers Burlingame was elected vice-president and put in charge of the company's operations. The man who had been the undertaker for Packard would now reluctantly perform the same role for Studebaker. Plan B was ready for operation. The Board recognized that if Studebaker were suddenly to terminate its auto operations, its dealer organization would flood the company with lawsuits. But, if the company could ensure the continuation of a supply of Studebaker cars of some type, at least for a time, the dealers would have no case. Churchill was put in charge of a task force to see if a German car could be secured for sale under the Studebaker nameplate. There was also the question of large defense and other government contracts which were scheduled for South Bend production. Should the company continue defense

operations in South Bend, even if auto production was ended? Two factors would prevent this. First, the banks, while they were willing to finance the present government production, they would not finance future contracts. More important was the matter of 30 million dollars in unfunded pension costs for the South Bend workers. If the corporation continued some operations in South Bend beyond the present union contract which would expire the next year, would the union insist that the company continue to pay into the pension fund? As it turned out, the union would so insist. The company decided it would have to sell off the defense contract and end all South Bend operations.

During the next two weeks, Guthrie, Burlingame, MacMillan, and others made one last survey of the South Bend situation to see if there was any possibility of staving off Plan B. They concluded the cause was hopeless. On Saturday, December 7th, the union officials were called in and apprised of the situation. On Monday the 9th, the workers returned to the plant to resume production after a two-week lay-off. When the line shut down at noon, many of them went out for lunch at the local beaneries. At the gates they found the reporters and television crews who gave them the news that Studebaker would close South

Bend auto production by the end of the month. In spite of the rumors of the previous weekend, many of them did not believe it; one of them told a reporter: "Studebaker will be here when you're dead and gone."

The company expected that its last few weeks of production would be beset by all manner of labor problems, including deliberate sabotage. It did not happen. A few weeks later, the last South Bend Studebaker, a red Daytona, came off the assembly line consigned to a dealer in Pennsylvania. In a final gesture of sentiment, the company kept the car, and it is now in the Studebaker Museum in South Bend. The following May a Studebaker worker who had been with the company since 1929 and who had worked in Department 154s body repair and stayed on the job after the close of assembly operation until all the cars were out of the plant stood at the Broadway gate. He looked up at the now silent plant and pronounced an epitaph for the Studebaker workers: "On the last day, just before I checked out, I went up to the second floor and walked along the empty assembly line. Everything was still in place, and I thought, 'we could start production tomorrow.' I couldn't believe there would never be a tomorrow."

Epilogue: Canada (1964-1966)

With the decision to close South Bend, the question of securing a Studebaker car for the dealers became all-important. Churchill concluded that a German car could not be obtained in time, and the decision was made to continue operations on the 1964 Studebaker model at Hamilton. The Hawk, Avanti, and truck production were all dropped, and only the Lark continued. Gordon Grundy, head of the Canadian operations, was put in charge of the effort. He was given to understand that the company would make an all-out effort to remain in business in Canada and that the future of Studebaker automotive was in his hands. He left the meeting in a state of euphoria. Whether top management was really thinking in terms of a continuing operation in Canada is problematical.

Gordon Grundy

When Grundy left the meeting, a Studebaker official who was present turned to Burlingame and said, "Byers, you know this can't be a continuing operation." Burlingame did not reply.

Grundy had some reason to be hopeful. Breakeven for the Canadian operation was only 7,000 units per year, and the plant had produced as many as 18,000 units on a one shift basis, and could produce 30,000 on two shifts. But all that was when the Canadian operation had been tied to South Bend. With South Bend closed, the small Canadian operation would have to carry sales overhead not only for Canadian marketing, but for the U.S. as well. Further, with reduced volume, suppliers who had calculated piece prices on the much larger demands of South Bend, began to clamor for an increase in prices. Engines were another problem.

The Studebaker Canadian Lark

1966 Studebaker Sliding-Roof Wagonaire Kamp King Coach featured a full kitchen, dinette; cupboard, closet and drawer space. It accomodated in-car sleeping for a family of five. A foldable vinyl door provided privacy for adults. It weighed 800 lbs and was reputed to have a 65 mph safe cruising speed.

49

For the first few months of production, the engine line was kept going at South Bend, but with the end of the union contract there, the company had to seek an outside supplier. The cost of South Bend engines had been $190 for a six and $214 for an eight. GM now offered to sell engines to Studebaker at $315 for a six and $434 for an eight. Finally GM agreed to furnish engines at "only" $130 above what they had cost in South Bend. The result of all this was to raise the Canadian breakeven point to 14,000 units per year.

In spite of these difficulties, Grundy bent every effort to make the Canadian operation a success. In March of 1964 he double shifted the plant, and looked around for ways to increase the automotive profits. Two of them were quite ingenious. One was for the importation of a Japanese make for sales by Studebaker dealers. The deal was on the verge of completion when, in Grundy's view, it was wrecked by the interference of one of Guthrie's law partners. The partner was Richard Nixon. Grundy's second plan was for Studebaker to serve as the importing agent for Volkswagon. The agreement allowed Volkswagon to avoid the payment of Canadian tariffs. The opposition parties in the Canadian Parliament considered it a piece of chicanery, and forced the government to bring it to an end. Grundy was now back to trying to turn a profit on Studebaker production, and he did continue to make small profits. The trouble was that the corporation was no longer willing to be satisfied with a small profit—it believed it had to make a profit commensurate with the investment in the Canadian plant and the sales operation. In 1965 Grundy was ordered not to add any more dealers, and not to replace those who terminated. He finally came to the reluctant conclusion that the company did not wish him to succeed. Nevertheless in February of 1966 he asked for funds to tool the 1967 model. His request was under $30-0,000. The company's answer was that there would be no 1967 production, and less than a month later, Hamilton produced the last Studebaker. It was the end of 114 years on the road.

Why Did It Happen?

Since the mid 1960s, historians, journalist, car buffs, and the public have tried to find the reasons for Studebaker's failure in the auto business. The most frequent explanation has been the unwillingness or the inability of the company to solve its labor costs. Certainly this was a prime factor until 1954, but at least by 1959, this problem had been substantially solved, and was not a significant factor in the 1960s. Another explanation is that Studebaker suffered from bad management, that, as one Studebaker official put it, whenever Studebaker came to a fork in the road, they took the wrong fork. There is little evidence of this. In the history of Studebaker from 1945 to 1966, only two really bad decisions were made. The first was the Packard merger, which did not save Packard, and put Studebaker in a financial hole from which it never really recovered. The second decision (or lack of decision) was the incredible manner in which management allowed its body rust problems to persist from 1953 to 1966 without a serious attempt to solve them. Still another factor was what might best be termed circumstances. Studebaker was the victim of extremely bad luck at crucial times, and almost never had a lucky break. In 1941 and again in 1950, war ended or curtailed auto production when the company was at its zenith. Steel and supplier strikes almost invariably came at the worst possible times. And the 1953-55 production race between Ford and GM, which was of no advantage to either company, nearly bankrupted Studebaker. In all its twenty-one post-war years, the company's only good luck was the post-World War II sellers' market, the 1959 Lark, and the surprising upturn in sales in 1961. A fourth factor in the demise of auto operations was the acquisitions program. So long as Studebaker was only in the automobile business it had only two choices: make cars or go broke. The acquisition policy got seriously underway in 1958 as a means of taking advantage of the company's tax credits and as a means of cushioning the swings in the auto market. From the point of view of auto operations it was too successful, for it made it possible for the company to go out of the automobile business without going bankrupt. But through the acquisitions policy the Board of

Studebaker Plant in Hamilton, Canada

Directors did save the company, and that is the job of a Board of Directors. A fifth factor was the refusal of the financial community to give Studebaker the necessary credit to bring out new models in 1962 or 1964. But the financial community put up the money for the Studebaker-Packard merger, agreed to financial rearrangements in 1956 and 1958, and financed the Franklin acquisition. In light of its experience with Studebaker, the financial community could hardly be blamed for its decisions of the 1960s. This brings us to a sixth and final factor. It was not that Studebaker could not make cars, but that they could not sell them. From 1954 on, the continual attrition of the dealer organization could be no more than temporarily reversed. Studebaker simply could not attract dealers of the quality of the Big Three or even of AMC. Within its limited means the company made strenuous efforts to do so, but in the end it was forced to recognize the dilemma: without new models it could not attract new dealers; without new dealers it could not sell enough cars to risk the future of the company by bringing out new models.

All this is the South Bend story. What about Canada? Could Studebaker have remained in auto business there without serious financial risk, at least for the foreseeable future. The answer is probably yes. But it must be remembered that Studebaker was now something new in American business: it was a conglomerate corporation. And for a conglomerate, the question it must put to each of its division is not are you breaking even, but are you making enough money to justify an investment that could be more profitable elsewhere? That was the bottom line for Studebaker of Canada. The Studebaker management gave the inevitable answer.

The history of Studebaker is the story of a single company and of the people from presidents to assembly line workers who tried to make it go. But it is more than that. In microcosm, it is the story of the American automobile industry in the first seven decades of this century. And therein lies its real importance.

BYERS A. BURLINGAME
PRESIDENT

Studebaker
CORPORATION

December 16, 1963

To All Studebaker Employees:

The decision by the Board of Directors to shut down
South Bend automobile assembly was a difficult one to
make. They had no other choice. With the high rate
of losses and the drop-off in sales volume, it was not
possible to continue to operate in facilities geared to
high-volume production.

To reduce our automotive operations in South Bend would
have cost millions of dollars -- dollars which are not
available to us.

We were faced with either complete abandonment of the
automobile business or quickly cutting our operations
to a size which would economically justify our remaining
in the business. The only possible way we could continue was to shut down most of South Bend and increase
our Canadian production.

The fact that this move allowed us to continue employing
a few hundred people is little consolation to those of
you who will no longer work here. I assure you that
we will cooperate with other employers who are interested
in hiring our people and with the efforts being made at
all levels to provide employment in this area. We have
publicly stated our regard for you, your years of
experience, and your ability.

It is heartening to note that the community, the state,
and the nation have promised to do whatever is possible
to alleviate the unemployment which inevitably occurs
as a result of this move.

You have stayed with us through many troubled times,
and on behalf of myself and the company I represent,
I want to express my heartfelt thanks.

Sincerely,

B. A. Burlingame

PART
III.
The Aftermath

MICHAEL BEATTY

The Workers

What happened when the Studebaker Corporation shut down its automotive division in South Bend? The initial worker reaction was a sense of disbelief. The story had been leaked and as the workers left for lunch on Monday, December 9, 1963, many refused to believe what the gathering group of television reporters and newspaper people were telling them. They had been through too many ups and downs with the plant to believe it was all over—for most much of their work history had been spiralling periods of high wages and more than equal periods of lay off. Lester Fox, Union vice president at the time, remarked that Studebaker workers "were unemployed too much to be working and working too much to be unemployed." Many of them had grown up with the plant, had family who had worked there for generations—60 percent had a family member who was still working there. Something that old, that big, "you don't believe it can die."

At its peak Studebaker had employed more than 22,000 workers in South Bend. Of the more than 7,000 working in 1963 the average age was 54. Almost half of these workers were unskilled, many had never worked for another employer. The plant was home to them, a part of the family. An internal personnel memo written by S.T. Skrentay to C.T.

Gallagher during the final days of work is worth quoting at length:

"To the individual employee the closing of the South Bend operations is an event without parallel. It is not like a model change over period. It is not the same as two successive down weeks... The difference is—as the sportscasters are fond of saying about a play-off game—there is no tomorrow. No one was prepared for this kind of a shock. The possibility that the South Bend operation could collapse was a chunk of reality that was never allowed to creep into the individual employee's mind; it never figured in his planning. If a mood permeates the work force—it is the mood of despair and disillusionment. It is also a mood of frustration, a frustration born of the fact that human experience had not prepared the average employee—especially the older worker whose future appears particularly bleak—with the tools to cope with the catastrophe he now sees a his future."

Further in the memo the worker's relationship with the company is discussed.

"To many, Studebaker—and you can forget about the divisions because they're not Studebaker—was more than a place of employment. Studebaker was really a member of the family—a capricious and wayward member—but a member nonetheless. . These people are thankful for what Studebaker has provided—and if you can't say anything nice about the dead than say nothing."

The eight Wilk Brothers, Stanley, Julius, Joseph, Frank, Chick, Benny, Ted, and Henry, all worked for Studebaker in 1952.

It is surprising that most workers felt that way, and still do feel that way about Studebaker. Velma Bokon Sikorski was part of a promotional film which the company produced for their 100th anniversary in 1952. The production was called "A Family of Craftsmen", and featured her family—brothers, sisters, and father—all working for the automotive manufacturer. Surprisingly, even though the shut-down broke up her family, she does not blame the company and remembers it fondly: "We were always proud to work for Studebaker, and even though they did close, you kind of have a bond with something like that. I worked at other places and I don't have that bond with the other places like I do with Studebaker."

The closing was not the only burden these workers had to accept. How could they go home and explain that they were permanently unemployed? At age 54 how could they go to school? How could they go on a job interview when, for many, that experience was half a lifetime away.

For some there was depression, alcoholism, and suicide. For most there was family or outside help. One of these was another member of "A Family of Craftsmen", Velma's brother, Rudy Bokon. Rudy thought his life was finished at age 46. His wife, Evelyn, remembers how she helped him: "Rudy said he was too old, and I said he wasn't... he was very depressed... so I just went down to the employment office and talked to Mrs. Battles and Mrs. Wolf and they said 'Evelyn, there are two openings at South Bend Lathe, and I'll give you a card and you tell Rudy to get over there tomorrow.' So the next day I took him there and he's been there ever since."

Photo Courtesy: *The South Bend Tribune*

Workers leaving the Plant on December 9, 1963, the day Studebaker announced it was going out of the automotive business in South Bend.

Help also came from outside the family. There was a vast outpouring of publicity, both on the local and national levels, about what was happening in South Bend. Bill Aramony, executive director of the local United Way in 1964, summed up people's feelings when he said publicly that the Studebaker workers had been good and faithful citizens of the community, and now, in their hour of need, the community would not turn its back on them. Assistance came pouring in from all over.

President Johnson created an interdepartmental committee which was committed to helping South Bend recover. The Secretary of Commerce, through the Area Redevelopment Administration, helped attract new business to the area. The Secretary of Agriculture liberalized eligiblity requirements to permit surplus food distribution to the displaced workers. The Secretary of Defense worked to see that the $87 million military truck contract that Studebaker had relinquished stayed in South Bend. The Secretary of Labor pushed to establish training programs. Indiana Senators Vance Hartke and Birch Bayh and local Congressman John Brademas helped push the project and hold it together.

South Bend became one of the first cities in the nation to take advantage of the federally funded Manpower Development and Training Act. In less than three years over 2,500 trainees were graduated and the plan was so successful that the community built Ivy Tech, the area vocational school, making use of funds from the Vocational Education Act of 1963—a bill which had as a sponsor Congressman Brademas.

The above photograph was taken during the production of the film: **"A Family of Craftsmen,"** a promotional piece for Studebaker which featured the Bokon family—most of whom worked, or had worked for Studebaker. Pictured at left is Velma Bokon Sikorski and her family. Mrs. Sikorski, and Rudy and Evelyn Bokon, are included in the family dinner portrait above.

Project ABLE—Ability Based On Long Experience—was a coordinated effort of the Department of Labor and the National Council on Aging. It was designed to assist Studebaker workers over the age of 50. The program was well administered by former union leader Lester Fox. Fox felt that the older worker, "at least those I've had experience with, are proud, they work hard to maintain their independence. When they have a need to ask for assistance, it is a genuine need, and one I find tremendous satisfaction in trying to fulfill." And fulfill it he has; the success of project ABLE helped in the creation of the social service agency Real Services. This organization still helps older adults and continues to expand—in 1984 the budget was almost $8 million. The Executive Director is Les Fox.

The result of all that effort was considered an unparalled success. In November, 1963, one month before the closing, unemployment in South Bend was at a recorded low of 2.1 percent. By the beginning of 1964 it had climbed to over 9 percent. By September of 1966 unemployment had been reduced to 2.3 percent, below the rates for Indiana and for the nation. Total employment was 104,000, a gain of more than 10,000 from the figure in January, 1961. As **Business Week** reported on February 19, 1966, South Bend's "major problem is a labor shortage."

Workers' personal stories, at least in part, were also successes. Perhaps it was the outpouring of assistance, or that special bond to Studebaker, that helped them through the hard times. Many of the workers did seem well prepared for their lay off. According to the **Business Week** article: "About 27 percent moonlighted (compared to a national average of 5 percent), 34 percent had working spouses, and 35 percent had non-wage sources of income such as dividends or veteran's benefits. About 72 percent had money in the bank before the shut down, and 65 percent still had it six months later. Only 3 percent were forced to return items purchased on credit." What these figures don't tell us is what happened to the rest of the workers, or the ones who had to radically change retirement plans.

Not all workers recovered, or recovered completely. Many older workers could not, or would not, learn new skills. Sociologists and economists such as Dr. Charles Craypo, who studied the Studebaker and other South Bend plant closings, found increased natural deaths, suicides, divorces, alcoholism, and other social and health problems among displaced workers.

The City

How did the city react to the closing? It did not "roll over and play dead", nor did it become the ghost town predicted by national television, even though many local people did share that prediction. To combat these psychological feelings of defeat and to help in recovery the recently elected mayor, Lloyd M. Allen, created a mayor's committee. Named to co-chair that committee were two business leaders with a long history of help to the community. Franklin D. Schurz was editor and publisher of the **South Bend Tribune** and had been the first to chair the Committee of 100—a business group formed in 1953 to help bring new business to the community. Paul D. Gilbert was a clothing retailer and was well known for his statement: "This is not Studebaker, Indiana. This is South Bend, Indiana."

And South Bend, Indiana it was. By the time it closed down the automotive operation in South Bend, Studebaker was only employing about 8 percent of the work force; the Bendix Corporation had taken the leadership as the largest employer. The Committee of 100 had done its job well. Between 1953 and 1963 more than 50 new businesses had moved into the area—this helped diversify the economic base and soften the blow which the closing dealt the city.

Within two years the darkest days in the city's history, at least the darkest days psychologically, were over. In real economic terms there had been worse times. During the recession of the 1950s South Bend had suffered through unemployment—in 1954 it rose to 19 percent—more than double that following the automotive shutdown. Part of the

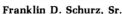

Franklin D. Schurz, Sr.

Paul D. Gilbert

recovery was the result of an upward moving national economy, but most of the credit should be shared by the community, government, and private agencies. Similar results would, at least, be questionable in the economy of 1983-84. Publicity would certainly not be as great because of the similar plight currently shared by industrial cities across the Northeast.

But Congressman John Brademas had reason to be proud when he spoke before Congress on October 12, 1966. Summing up the feelings of the community he reported that "South Bend has truly come back. Because of our magnificent economic recovery we are now enjoying a period of unprecedented growth and prosperity... I believe that other communities in the United States which have the misfortune to lose a major industry will benefit

from studying the South Bend story. It proves with certainty that federal, state, and local governments and community leaders can work efficiently and effectively together in times of crisis."

Through hindsight many people view the close of automotive operations as a blessing in disguise. No longer did automotive industry fluctuations play a major role in the economic life of the area. The city was able to shake the poor labor image of the past; and a diversified industrial base meant a stronger community.

But not everyone saw it, or sees it, as a blessing. Many employees had to take jobs below their skill level, as well as below their former wage level. Lost pensions meant changed retirement plans. Because workers had to relocate, families were broken up. For South Bend manufacturing was replaced by the service industry, which meant lower wages and a lower tax base.

South Bend's skyline had changed by 1981. The taller structures, from left, are the County-City Building, The Odd Fellows Building (demolished in 1983), The American Valley Bank Building, The JMS Building (named for John M. Studebaker), and at the far right The First Bank Center (under construction).

South Bend Recovers

What is the city like twenty years after the shut down? To understand South Bend, one must understand Michiana; which is generally defined geographically as Barrien and Cass Counties in Michigan and LaPorte, St. Joseph, Elkhart, Starke, and Marshall Counties in Indiana. South Bend is the nucleus of this area which boasts a population larger than the states of Alaska, Wyoming, Vermont, and Delaware. It also produces more general merchandise retail sales than the states of Vermont, Wyoming, North and South Dakota and Alaska. As the hub of an area this size South Bend's movement toward a retail and service economy is understandable. In 1984, two of the three largest employers are the University of Notre Dame and the health industry—the three hospitals in South Bend employed close to 3,000 workers at the beginning of 1984. Twenty years after South Bend's image industry shutdown, the economy was at a six year high with cautious optimism for steady and reasonable growth.

The population of the city is down. One prediction shows a slowly declining population with no growth until after the beginning of the twenty-first century and a population in 2,020 less than the population in 1970. However, the population of the region is growing, and projections show

it continuing to do so. There is a new Committee of 100 called Project Future. Its goals are familiar: to strengthen local business, assist business expansions, support entrepreneurial efforts, and attract outside business to the community. So far Project Future has been a success, by 1984 it had aided in the creation of over 3,000 jobs in new and expanding firms. The city looks good. Much urban renewal has taken place, with varying levels of success. One of South Bend's major assets—the St. Joseph River—is being developed. The city seems to be working towards the potential as the cultural and entertainment center of the region, as well as its economic and geographic hub.

What would happen today if another major corporation were to leave South Bend? When asked that question, Jack Powers, the managing editor of the **South Bend Tribune**, responded: "The community would be in a lot better shape to handle it... a lot more calmly, with a better sense of direction, a better sense of what can't be accomplished as well as what can be accomplished... I think the community would handle it a lot better."

Photo Courtesy: *The South Bend Tribune*, Joe Raymond

South Bend today shows continuing development with new cultural and financial centers.

Studebaker and Conclusions

What happened to Studebaker after it shut down automotive operations in South Bend? After dropping the automotive division in South Bend, Studebaker made a profit. In 1966 automotive production was shut down in Canada and Studebaker went out of the automotive industry completely. In 1967 the company merged again and became the Studebaker-Worthington Corporation. There was an office in South Bend until 1977, but by that time Studebaker's commitment to the community had been reduced to two employees. In October of 1979 the McGraw-Edison Company absorbed the corporation and, because Studebaker no longer referred to a specific product, the name was dropped and disappeared from American business.

There are many lessons to learn from Studebaker and from South Bend. Lessons for industries, communities, and individuals. Although the final outcome seems positive—depending upon how one gauges human suffering, any human suffering—most workers did receive other jobs, stock owners made a profit, bank loans were paid, and the community recovered. South Bend was lucky. Many cities in the Northern Industrial Corridor have not been as lucky and this raises serious questions about the responsibilities of companies and the social costs to individuals and communities. Perhaps Studebaker still has a contribution to make, as an example and case study for the present and the future.